Venus of Barcelona. History Museum of Barcelona.

toric, monumental and artistic patrimony, centred above all in two fundamental nuclei: the Gothic Quarter, containing the cathedral, the city hall, and the Palau de la Generalitat, seat of the autonomous government of Catalonia; and the works of the inimitable Modernist architect Antoni Gaudí, most of whose most remarkable creations are to be found in Barcelona. These include the Sagrada Família, the Park Güell and "La Pedrera". Moreover, the important cultural and artistic inheritance of the city means that it can also offer the visitor a large number of museums, two of the finest of which are the Picasso Museum and the Catalan Art National Museum.

For decades, partly due to the industrial expansion of the mid-20th century, the city lived "with its back to the sea", until the designation of Barcelona as host city to the 1992 Olympic Games (considered the finest in the modern history of the Games) provided the opportunity to regain contact with the sea through the restoration of its coastline. The Port of Barcelona is now one of the most important of the entire Mediterranean, and its coasts offer five kilometres of beach.

"Commentaries on Social Customs and Practices" (Jaume Marquilles, 15th century). History Museum of Barcelona.

3

The Cathedral.

Central Nave of the Cathedral. ▷

The Cathedral and the Gothic Quarter

Barcelona Cathedral began to be built in 1298, on the site of a former Romanesque cathedral which, it is thought, had in turn been constructed on the placement of a Paleo-Christian chapel dating back to the 4th century. The Gothic building was completed in 1459, though the main front and the dome were not added until the late-19th century. Inside, under the presbytery, is the **Crypt of Santa Eulàlia**. This has a curious vault, almost completely flat in shape and divided into two arches, under which is the tomb of the saint, dating back to the 14th century and supported by smooth alabaster columns. Also interesting in the Cathedral interior are the **choirstalls**, with fine painting and precious metalwork, and the **Chapterhouse**, where is displayed the statue of the Sant Crist of Lepant, which accompanied John of Austria at the battle of Lepanto. Next to the high altar of the cathedral (con-

BARCELONA

Text, photographs, design, lay-out and
printing completely created by
the technical department of
EDITORIAL ESCUDO DE ORO S.A.

All total or partial reproduction and
translation rights reserved.

Copyright of this edition on photographs and literary text:
© EDITORIAL ESCUDO DE ORO S.A.
Palaudàries, 26 - 08004 Barcelona (Spain).

www.eoro.com
e-mail: editorial@eoro.com

Editorial Escudo de Oro, S.A.

Roman Temple of Augustus.

INTRODUCTION

For more than 4,000 years, a history in which it has been occupied by many different cultures, Barcelona has always stood out for its beauty and dynamism. Over the centuries, the city has become rightly famed for its industriousness and modernity, qualities which have again and again made it a pioneer, and a city of prodigious feats.

Since time immemorial, Barcelona has always taken full advantage of its position as a coastal city to reach overseas for the riches and opportunities offered by the outside world. The greatest moments in the city's history were during medieval times, when it was a prosperous trading centre, and in the 19th century, when it enjoyed enormous economic and demographic growth which in 1859 forced the demolition of the city walls which had previously prevented its expansion. This flourishing period culminated in the organisation of the universal exhibitions of 1888 and 1929, historic dates which were also key events in determining the appearance and layout of the city. Barcelona also possesses an enormous, rich his-

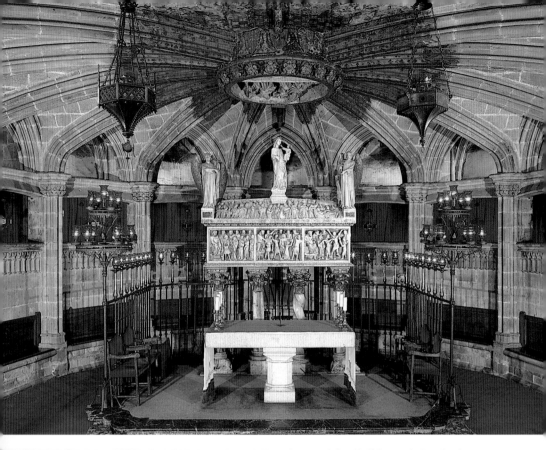

Crypt of St. Eulàlia and detail of the vault keystone, dedicated to the "The Virgin of Compassion".

secrated in 1337) is a splendid wooden altarpiece dating back to the 15th century. The cathedral can be entered by various gates: the **Porta de Sant Iu**, the oldest of these, which stands in carrer dels Comtes, and those of **Santa Eulàlia**, **Santa Llúcia** and **la Pietat (Mercy)**. All of these give access to the lovely 14th-century **cloisters** surrounded by chapels facing into the central courtyard. Adjoining the cloisters is the **Chapel of Santa Llúcia**, dating back to 1268. Barcelona Cathedral was declared Historic-Artistic Monument of National Interest in 1929.

All around the cathedral are numerous beautiful buildings, many of them of outstanding importance in the history of the city and which together make up the historic centre of Barcelona, known as the **Gothic Quarter**. As soon as you come out of the cathedral, in the Pla de la Seu, you are confronted with the **Pia Almoina** (Pious Alms, from the 15th century, built to house this charitable institution), which today is the site of the **Diocese Museum**. Along the contiguous street called Comtes you come to Plaça Sant Iu, which is the location of the **Frederic Marès Museum**. This museum contains the collections put together by this artist and

Door of Mercy, chapel of St. Llúcia and cloister.

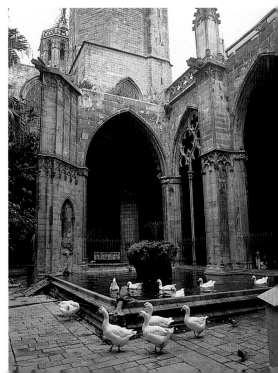

Plaça del
Rei and
Frederic
Marès
Museum.

Ardiaca ▷
House and
modernist
detail in the
entrance.

Tinell Ceremonial Room.

Chapel of St. Agueda. ▷

two particularly important exhibitions are: the section on sculptures, with pieces dating from the pre-Roman period up to the beginning of the 20th century; and the other which is a collection of everyday objects. A few steps further on is the historical **Plaça del Rei** (Square of the King), a medieval nucleus comprising the **Palau del Lloctinent** (Royal Lieutenants's Palace, dating from the 15th century although it was remodelled in the 19th century), the **Torre-mirador del rei Martí** (King Martin's Watch Tower, built in 1555), the **Palau Reial Major** (Main Royal Palace, dating back to the 11th century and which contains the Tinell Ceremonial Room), and the **Santa Àgueda Chapel** (Gothic chapel dating from the 14th century which holds the Retable of the Condestable, one of the most noteworthy pieces of Catalan Gothic painting). The visit to these last three buildings is included in a route suggested by the **History Museum of Barcelona** which is in Casa Padellàs, next to Plaça del Rei, and which also includes the plaza basement with Roman remains and the foundations of the cathedral from the Visigothic period.

Opposite the Chapel of Santa Llúcia (cathedral) is the **Ardiaca House**, forming a unique historic site with the **Dea-**

The Plaça
Sant Jaume
and Palau
de la
Generalitat.

Palau de la
Generalitat:
Gothic
cloister.

Bisbe Street: ▷
Neo-Gothic
bridge.

Barcelona City Council.

con's House, which began to be built in the 12th century over one section of the old Roman walls. Nearby is **Bisbe street**, in which the most outstanding buildings are the **Bishop's Palace** and the **Casa dels Canonges**. This narrow street opens out into the spacious **Plaça Sant Jaume** where stand, facing each other, the **City Hall** (containing such rooms as the Cent Room and the Sessions Chamber) and the **Palau de la Generalitat** (Saló de Sant Jordi and the courtyard known as the Pati dels Tarongers).

City Council building: Cent Room.

Picasso Museum and carrer Montcada

Carrer Montcada is a charming street whose origins go back to the 12th century, when the ruling classes decided to connect the district to the seaside zones of the city. During the 14th-18th centuries, carrer Montcada was the residence of the Barcelona aristocracy, and fine palaces were built all along it. As a result, the street is now a living monument to medieval civil architecture, unequalled anywhere else in the city for interest and quality. The **Picasso Museum** is much frequented and holds a well-rounded collec-

Entrance to the Picasso Museum, view of Montcada Street and the Marcús Chapel.

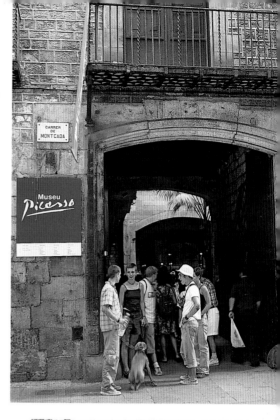

tion of his works. It is located in the old palaces of Berenguer d'Aguilar, the Baron of Castellet and Meca, and has been extended recently with the inclusion of the palace-houses Mauri and Finestres. The Picasso Museum was opened in 1963 with paintings by Picasso donated by Jaume Sabater, Picasso's friend. Some years later the collection was added to with contributions from Picasso himself and members of his family.

In Montcada street you will also find other palace-houses such as the **Casa de la Custòdia**, in front of the **Marcús Chapel** (Romanesque); the **Marquis of Llió Palace**, now the loca-

tion of the **Textile and History of Clothing Museum**; the **Nadal Palace**, location of the **Barbier-Mueller Museum of Pre-Columbian Art**; the **Dalmases Palace**, location of the **Omnium Cultural**, and the **Cervelló-Guidice Palace-House**, location of the **Maeght Gallery**. At the end of the street we come to Plaça de Santa Maria, dominated by the **Church of Santa Maria del Mar**, the finest of Catalan Gothic churches, built between 1329 and 1384, under the reign of Alfons IV, the Benign. In 1931 Santa Maria del Mar was designated a Historic-Artistic Monument of National Interest.

Church Santa Maria del Mar.

Main nave of Church Santa Maria del Mar.

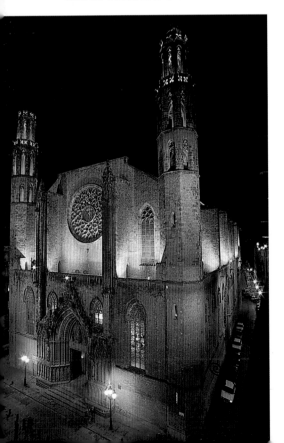

Plaça Catalunya and the Canaletes fountain.

The colourful Rambla

The Barcelona Rambla begins in **Plaça Catalunya**, considered the very centre of the city. Originally, the Rambla was a stream running along the city walls. In the 18th century, population growth made the city too small to house all its inhabitants and the walls were therefore demolished and a promenade constructed, now famous throughout the world. The central section of the Rambla is dotted with kiosks selling flowers, animals, and newspapers and magazines, by pave-

Bethlehem Church.

Virreina Palace.

ment cafés and, towards the end, by stands and stalls where craftsmen and women sell their wares, Tarot card readers offer their services and pavement artists show their skills (as in the nearby Plaça del Pi). At the top of the Rambla is the **Canaletes Fountain**, a 19th-century wrought-iron piece to which is attached the legend that all those who drink of its waters are certain to return to Barcelona.

A walk down the Rambla allows us to admire a number of fine examples of 18th-century civil architecture, such as the Royal Academy of Science and Art, now the **Poliorama Theatre**, the former seat of the **Compañía de Tabacos de Filipinas**, or the **Moja Palace** (adjoining the shop-lined Carrer Portaferrisa), once the home of the poet Verdaguer as the guest of the marquises of Comillas. Another interesting building is the **Bethlehem Church**, one of the few examples of Baroque architecture to be seen in the city. A short walk from the

Rambla, level with this church, is the former **Hospital of the Santa Creu**, a 15th-century site which now houses such institutions as the **Catalan Library**, the **Institute of Catalan Studies** and the **Academy of Medicine** (in the former Convalescent Home).

The **Virreina Palace** is another architectural jewel adorning the Rambla and is considered to be a model of perfection among 18th-century Catalan civil architecture. In 1941, the entire complex was declared a Historic-Artistic Monument of National Interest.

A little farther down the Rambla, we come to the popular **Market of the Boqueria** (or of Sant Josep), dating back to the 18th century and surprising both architecturally, as it is housed in a splendid Modernist building, and socially, due to its lively, colourful atmosphere. Homage is made to this market by the **Pla de l'Os**, by Miró, a work set into the pavement of the central area of the Rambla.

Patio of the Old Hospital of the Santa Creu.

Two views of the Ramblas.

Just before we enter the Plaça Reial, we can pause for a moment to admire the front of the pride of Barcelonan cultural society, the **Gran Teatre del Liceu**. It was first opened in 1847 but in 1994 the entire theatre interior was destroyed by fire and the only part of the building that was saved was the facade that looks on to the Ramblas.

After a period of intense rebuilding which included extending the building on its south face, the

Pla de l'Os: mosaic by Miró.

Gran Teatre del Liceu.

Güell Palace.

Gran Teatre del Liuceu was reopened in 1999.

The **Plaça Reial** is one of the city's most emblematic spaces. This lively square is flanked on all sides by tall buildings supported by arcades between whose archways are cafés, bars and restaurants. In the centre is the Fountain of the Tres Glòries and lamp posts with six brackets, designed by Gaudí.

Opposite this square, in Carrer Nou de la Rambla, is another architectural jewel: the **Güell Palace**, also designed by Gaudí. The interior features mosaic-lined fireplaces and arches. This palace was declared a Historic-Artistic Monument of National Interest in 1969, whilst in 1984 UNESCO listed it in its Catalogue of World Patrimony.

Almost ending our tour of the Ramblas, we now come to the 16th-century **Principal Theatre**, Barcelona's first theatre and which still conserves its original front. Finally, opposite the **Santa Mónica Arts Centre**, is one of the museums dearest to the hearts of the people of Barcelona, the **Wax Museum**, whose whose creation was inspired by the film director Enrique Alarcón and which is installed in an interesting 19th-century building.

Situated in the Raval ward, in one of the most completely renovated areas in Ciutat Vella district, is the **Museum of Contemporary Art of Barcelona (MACBA)**. The building, designed by Richard Meier, stands in Plaça dels Àngels. Its construction began in 1990 and was completed in the spring of 1995. The labyrinthine character of the area is in stark contrast with the complex architecture of the MACBA, with forms ranging from flat elements and rectilinear windows to curved and undulating spaces in consonance with the contemporary spirit of the museum collection. The museum exhibits works collected by the Fundació Museu d'Art Contemporani, enrichenet thanks to the contributions of the private sector and to a team which makes a visit to the museum obligatory for an understanding of the artistic and cultural scene in Barcelona.

Plaça Reial.

Drassanes (the shipyards).

Sant Pau del Camp, the Monument to Columbus and surrounding area

The original city sprang up by the sea, reaching its maximum moment of splendour during the Middle Ages, its shipyards turning out large vessels. Next to these shipyards is the starting-point of **Paral.lel Avenue**, one of the most famous thoroughfares of Barcelona, one which for years was the centre of entertainment and theatre. "Paral·lel", home of some of the oldest and best-loved theatres in Barcelona, such as El Molino (closed in 1999), Arnau Theatre and Apolo, also surprises us with the presence of the lovely **Church of Sant Pau del Camp**, founded in the 10th century as a Benedictine abbey and a magnificent example of 11th-century (and earlier, as it contains the tombstone of Wifred II, dating back to the year 912) Catalan Romanesque style. The cloisters are the only Catalan Romansque work with trefoiled arches. As far back as 1879 it was declared a Monument of National Interest.

Church of Sant Pau del Camp.

The Plaça del Portal Nou, on Barcelona's seafront (Passeig Marítim) is dominated by the **monument to Columbus**, commemorating that explorer's visit to the city after his discovery of America to report his findings to the Catholic Monarchs. The monument was erected to mark the occasion of the first Universal Exhibition, held in Barcelona in 1888. A lift takes visitors 87 metres up the column, which is crowned by a statue of

View of the port: Columbus monument and the Maremagnum leisure centre.

Church of La Mercè and statue of the lady patron of Barcelona.

Columbus. This point commands a splendid panoramic view of the city and the coast.

Close by are the **Drassanes (Shipyards)**, the finest of their type which can now be seen anywhere in the world. Dating back to the 14th century, in medieval times ships were built here which took part in some of the most spectacular sea battles of the age. The site now houses **Barcelona's Maritime Museum**, with vessels dating back to the 14th and 15th centuries. Not far from this site are the remains of part of the medieval city walls.

The monument to Columbus also marks the beginning of the Bosch i Alsina dock, better known as the **Moll de la Fusta** ("wood's dock") as it was here that wood was stored. It was only recently that this site was converted into a leisure area looking out to sea, whilst to the rear a fast ring-road was built.

Shielded from the sea, though so close to it, stands the **Church of La Mercè**, a basilica which in around 1835 formed part of a Mercedarian convent and which is now dedicated to the patron saint of the city, the Our Lady of Mercy ("La Mercè"), represented by a lovely Gothic statue kept inside the church.

In the same area, in a square adjoining Vía Laietana, is the monumental central **post office building** ("Correus"), dating back to the early-20th century. Overlooking the port, this building features two fine towers.

In the nearby Pla de Palau is the **Llotja**, or exchange, used as a goods store and busy trading centre in medieval times. The Llotja was declared a Historic-Artistic Monument of National Interest in 1931.

Opposite Passeig d'Isabel II are the **Porxos d'en Xifré**, whose base is made up of a series of 21 arches forming an arcade supporting a row of 3-storey buildings with balconied windows.

Finally, before leaving this area of the city, we should pay a visit to the **Barceloneta district**, an old fishing quarter which, in spite of the extensive alterations carried out in preparation for the Olympic Games, still retains much of its original atmosphere.

Post Office Building.

Aerial view of the Ciutadella Park.

The Ciutadella, an oasis of green

The **Ciutadella Park** is the second-largest gardened area in Barcelona. The park began to be built in 1871, on the site occupied by Philip V's troops, to provide the venue for the 1888 Universal Exhibition. The Ciutadella is made up of a series of paths and gardens arranged around the central Plaça de les Armes.

This square contains an oval pond presided over by "Desconsol" ("Grief"), the most famous of the works of the sculptor Josep Llimona. Nearby is the **Catalan Parliament** building and, in the centre of an esplanade, the **Font de la Cascada**, a French-style monumental fountain designed by Fontseré and Gaudí. Various other sculptures are also distributed throughout the park, such as the Romantic **Dama del Paraigües (The Lady of the umbrellas)**.

There are also various important science museums in the park, including the **Geological Museum** (the oldest in Bar-

"Desconsol", the work of Josep Llimona. Behind the sculpture is the Catalan Parliament building.

"Font de la Cascada" and-the Lady of the umbrellas.

Geology Museum and the Hivernacle.

Floquet de Neu (Snowflake).

celona), the **Zoological Museum**, housed in the former Exhibition café-restaurant, and the **Modern Art Museum**, adjoining the Catalan Parliament building in the Plaça de les Armes, former parade ground of the citadel.

Finally, **Barcelona Zoo** is also contained in the Ciutadella Park. This is one of the finest in Europe and is well worth a visit. The Zoo was founded in 1894 and its most illustrious guest was Snowflake, the albino gorilla, the only one of its type known in the world.

Just outside the park, providing a majestic entrance to Passeig de Lluís Companys, containing such fine buildings as the **Palace of Justice**, is the **Arch of Triumph**, also built for the 1888 Universal Exhibition. In bare brick, the arch features reliefs celebrating 19th century industry and trade. The main front is crowned by the royal coat of arms, under which is that of the city of Barcelona, forming the centre of a group of emblems of the Spanish provinces.

Arch of Triumph.

Aerial view of Serra House, today the headquarters of the provincial government.

Passeig de Gràcia: Modernist Barcelona

Plaça Catalunya, nerve centre of the city, is the starting-point of two promenades of which the people of Barcelona are especially fond: **Rambla de Catalunya** and **Passeig de Gràcia**. Both streets are filled not only with some of the most outstanding Modernist works, but also with a special, unmistakable atmosphere. Rambla de Catalunya is the continuation towards the mountain of the famous Rambla, described above, and is lined throughout with fashionable boutiques, jewellery shops and pavement cafés. Its outstanding buildings include the Modernist **Farmàcia J. de Bolós**, and **Serra House**, seat of the provincial government, an early 20th-century work by the architect Josep Puig i Cadafalch.

Nearby is the **Antoni Tàpies Foundation**, installed in another Modernist building, the formerly occupied by the Montaner i Simó publishing company. The foundation was created by the artist himself in

Rambla de Catalunya.

Antoni Tàpies Foundation.

Amatller House and Batlló House.

1984 in order to promote the study of modern art and to exhibit the work of contemporary artists. The front of the building is crowned by a metallic roof, originally constructed to palliate the differences in height with the adjoining buildings, but ably used in the service of art by Tàpies, as he made it the base for his wire sculpture Núvol i Cadira ("Cloud and Chair").

In **Passeig de Gràcia** is the block of houses known as the **Mançana de la Discòrdia**

("Apple of Discord"), due to the contrasting architectural styles of the house fronts. The first building is the **Lleó Morera House**, constructed by Domènech i Montaner in 1905. Its front features numerous sculptural elements and the building is crowned by a pavilion which was destroyed during the Spanish Civil War and restored in the 1980s by Oscar Tusquets and Carles Díaz. The decorative elements in the building, as well as its stained-glass windows, mosaics and floors, comprise a splendid illustration of the floral style of the Catalan Modernists.

Another of the buildings forming the "Apple of Discord" is the **Amatller House**, designed by Puig i Cadafalch in 1890 and built on the site of an earlier construction. Its colourful front is made up of overlapping elements reminiscent of foreign architectural styles, whilst the rest of the building is in Neo-Gothic style. The lobby of the building is adorned with a series of reliefs including allegories of the Fine Arts and a representation of Saint George and the dragon. In 1976, the Casa Amatller was declared Historic-Artistic Monument of National Interest.

The block is completed by the **Batlló House**, a building renovated by Gaudí for the textile magnate Josep Batlló. The building is easily recognisable due to the surprising undulating form of its balconies. The colourful front is adorned by ceramic and glass, providing a singular range of hues, and the steep roof, which conceals a garret, is presided over by

Lleó Morera House.

Milà House, "la Pedrera".

a tower featuring the anagram in golden letters of "Jesus, Mary and Joseph" and a four-sided cross. This house was also declared a Historic-Artistic Monument of National Interest in 1969.

Passeig de Gràcia also contains one of Antoni Gaudí's masterpieces, a construction which broke completely with the canons of conventional architecture and which is imbued throughout with the remarkable personality of its creator. We are referring to the **Milà House** (1905-10), popularly known as **La Pedrera** ("The Quarry"). The front of this building provides a splendid illustration of Gaudí's creative capacity, contrasting wrought iron from Vilafranca del Penedès with stone. The stones of undulating curves of the front form a self-supporting wall connected to the rest of the structure through curved girders, in a light, graceful creation. Inside are small air shafts, but no central staircase, so that access to the various floors is by lift or the service stairway. But the most unusual artistic forms are to be found on the roof: chimneys and ventilation outlets in white marble, decorated brick or coloured glass forming abstract figures reminiscent of surrealist art. The roof takes the form of marine flora and fauna. In 1969 the building was declared a Historical-Artistic Monument of National Interest and in 1984 UNESCO listed it in the catalogue of human patrimony. In 1986 the building was restored by the Fundació de la Caixa de Catalunya that now uses it as its headquarters using the first floor as an exhibition room and the dormer windows in the space dedicated to the work of Gaudí known as "**Espai Gaudí**".

At the junction with Diagonal Avenue is the **Casa de les Punxes** ("House of Points"), so named due to the sharp points crowning its towers, conferring it a certain Nordic air. This three-storey block of flats was constructed by Puig i Cadafalch in 1903, and has six fronts decorated with elements typical of the Nordic Gothic style in harmony with Spanish Mannerist devices.

Casa de les Punxes.

Three views of the Palau de la Música Catalana.

The Palau de la Música Catalana, home of culture

The Palau de la Música Catalana is a Modernist building built between 1905 and 1908 and which is the culminating work of the architect Domènech i Montaner. The palace was conceived as the seat and concert hall of the Orfeó Català, a choir founded in the late-19th century by Lluís Millet and Amadeu Vives and which played a fundamental role in popularising Catalan music. The "Palau" was quickly

incorporated into the cultural life of the city and became the natural venue for all expressions of national culture. Architecturally, it is fascinating to see how this huge building adapts to the layout of the labyrinth of narrow streets in which it stands. Its outstanding external feature is the sculptural group on the corner of the first floor, depicting Saint George in full armour and in combat position, surrounded by figures from daily life and a damsel representing Music. This work is considered a masterpiece of Catalan naturalist sculpture. Inside the building, we find marble columns and floors, immense staircases, rich decoration, wide windows with multi-coloured glass, ceramic, a lovely central skylight, an impressive organ over the stage, and much more. An army of artists lent their skills to the construction and decoration of the "Palau", creating a monument of ornamentation and harmony. The Palau de la Música Catalana was given the Building of the Year Award in 1909 by the Town Council of Barcelona, and in 1997 it was registered as part of the UNESCO World Heritage.

Details of the ornamentation in the Palau de la Música Catalana.

Pedralbes Palace.

Pedralbes and Tibidabo, the heights of the city

The **Pedralbes Palace** was constructed in 1921 by Bona i Puig and De Paula Nebot on a site owned by the Güell family as a residence for King Alfonso XIII, though due to the vagaries of Spanish history he was never to stay here. The palace was declared Historic-Artistic Monument of National Interest in 1931, at the same time as it became property of Barcelona City Council. It has been in public use since 1960, housing such collections as the **Ceramic Museum**, one of the most important of its type in Spain, with pieces dating as far back as the 12th century. In Pedralbes Avenue are the **Pavilions Güell**, another splendid palace designed by Gaudí, whose doors, walls and entrance pavilions can be admired today.

The **Monastery of Pedralbes** is a beautiful, harmonious jewel of 14th-century architecture. It houses a collection of 16th-century art and furniture, as well as the **Thyssen-Bornemisza Collection**. The site was declared of National Interest in 1931.

This area is bordered by **Mount Tibidabo**, whose summit is occupied by a funfair, in existence for 100 years.

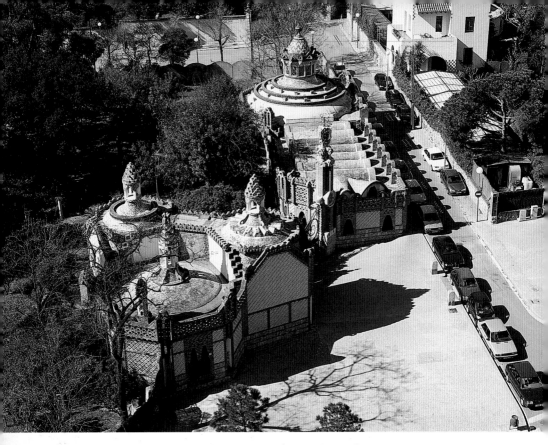

Güell
Pavilions.

Pedralbes
Monastery.

The Sacred ▷
Heart
Temple in
Tibidabo.

Main stairs in Güell Park.

Three views of Güell Park.

The dreams of Gaudí: Güell Park and Sagrada Família

Güell Park: Eusebi Güell had the original idea, commissioning Gaudí with its execution. The plan was to build an English-style garden city with 60 one family houses. In the end, only two of these were built, the architect himself living in one. Gaudí's creative genius conceived an architectural space which existed in communion with nature.

At the entrance to the park is a wide double flight of steps featuring waterfalls and sculptures, including a multi-colour, mosaic-covered dragon. This relatively small element has become one of the symbols of the park, along with the 100-columned chamber (only 84 were finally built) which supports the huge undulating square, whose balconies are also decorated with mosaics.

Sagrada Família: another of the most emblematic symbols of Barcelona, and one of its most-visited sights. Gaudí began to direct work on this temple in 1883, intending it to be the great modern church of Barcelona, and

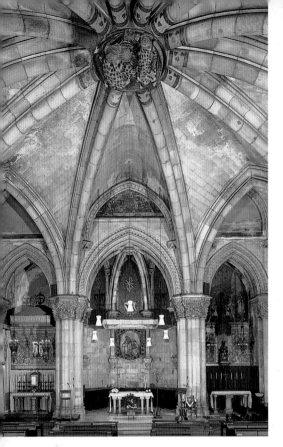

Sagrada Família Crypt.

Sagrada Família relief, in the crypt altar, the work of Josep Llimona.

Gaudí Avenue.

designing a complex system of Christian symbols to be represented in its construction. The project consisted of a nave and four aisles with transept and apse and an exterior ambulatory, with 18 large parabolic towers symbolising the 12 apostles, the four evangelists, the Virgin Mary and Jesus Christ (to be represented by the highest tower). The belltowers or spires, slightly convex in form and each containing a spiral staircase are

Birth facade.

Passion facade.

Hospital de la Santa Crei i Sant Pau.

engraved with texts which are repeated both horizontally and vertically. The pinnacles crowning them are splendid examples of the surrealist imagination of Gaudí, and are covered in multi-coloured vitreous mosaics and crowned by spectacular crosses. Gaudí's complete plans and a number of models can be seen in the **Museum of Sagrada Familia**, situated under the four towers of the Front of the Passion. Leaving the Cathedral of the Sagrada Família, we take Gaudí Avenue until we come to the **Hospital de la Santa Creu i Sant Pau**, whose site occupies the equivalent of nine blocks in Barcelona's Eixample district. This hospital was built by the architect Lluís Domènech i Montaner who, in order to show his disgust with the grid-like pattern of the Cerdà Plan, oriented the buildings diagonally to the planned layout of the new district. The design includes pavilions devoted to different medical specialisations, joined by underground galleries and surrounded by what was originally conceived as a large gardened area.

Monument dedicated to the "Sardana" in Montjuïc.

Montjuïc and the Olympic Ring

The mountains of Montjuïc and Tibidabo are the two mountains that surround Barcelona. Montjuïc mountain is divided up into a series of areas with different characteristics, and it is worth taking your time visiting each one. Most of these areas were developed as a result of two events the gained the city worldwide recognition: the World Expo, 1929; and the 1992 Olympic Games, the culmination of the urban development of the mountain. Fruit of the World Expo 1929 are: **National Palace**, **Spanish Town**, the **"Magic Fountain"**, and the **Mies van der Rohe Pavilion** (this building has been described by experts as the "paradigm of modern architecture"). The many and distinct buildings of the **Olympic Ring** are the result of the 1992 Olympic Games urban development. But, Montjuïc also houses a fair number of museums as well as gardens. Among the latter those that particularly stand out are the: **Costa i Llobera Gardens; Mossèn Cinto Verdaguer Gardens;** and the **Institute-Botanical Gardens**, which specialises in flora from the five regions of the world with a Mediterranean climate.

The CaixaForum Cultural Center.

Montjuïc Castle.

Miró Foundation.

The construction of **Montjuïc Castle** dates back to the second half of the 18th century and has as its famous precursor a fortress built in just 30 days during the Guerra dels Segadors ("War of the Reapers") in 1640. The castle now contains an interesting **Military Museum**.

The **Miró Foundation** also has its seat on Montjuïc. The building is a rationalist, one-storey construction, designed during the 1970s by Josep Lluís Sert, a friend of the artist. The different rooms making up the Foundation are grouped around a central courtyard and are illuminated naturally through rooflights. The Foundation was created by Miró himself in 1971 and has two missions: to promote the study and popular understanding of the artist's work.

CaixaForum, a large cultural center, is a very recent creation that has been installed in the old modernist textile factory Casa Ramona, a work by Puig i Cadafalch in 1908, situated at the beginning of the avenue Marqués de Comillas. Since its inauguration in 2002, it has become one of the most visited art centers in the city. Its rooms house the contemporary art collection of La Caixa Foundation, who manage the

Olympic Stadium and Palau Sant Jordi.

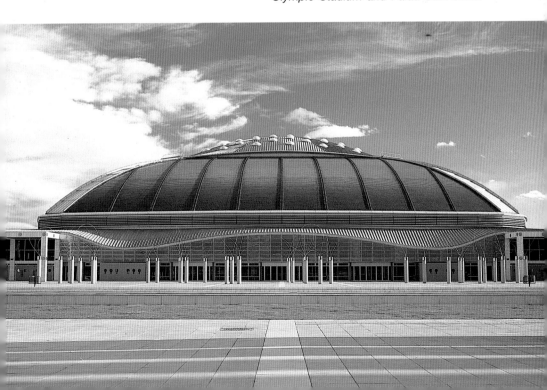

Main square in Spanish Town.

Pantocrator (12th century), in the MNAC. ▷

center, and the temporary exhibits of international renown.

Continuing our tour of the mountain, in Estadi Avenue we find the **Olympic Ring**, made up of the buildings especially constructed or rehabilitated for the 1992 Olympic Games as the **Olympic Stadium**. The facilities include the **Palau Sant Jordi**, a 17,000-seater sports hall constructed by the Japanese architect Arata Isozaki and featuring (particularly the roof), the most advanced techniques.

Poble Espanyol (Spanish Town) was built for the 1929 Universal Exhibition as a synthesis of Spanish archi-

tecture. This picturesque "village" forms a display of the most representative styles from the various areas of Spain, such as the walls of Avila, a reproduction of which surrounds the enclosure.

However, perhaps most impressive sight on Montjuïc is the **National Palace**, also constructed in 1929 for the Universal Exhibition. This is a grandiose, monumental building, eclectic in style and crowned by a majestic dome with a smaller cupola at either end and 4 towers reminiscent of those of Santiago de Compostela. In 1934, the Palau Nacional was converted into the seat of the **Catalan**

EGO SVM LVX MVDI

EE:S MRIA S IOANES

Reina Maria Cristina Avenue. In the background, Tibidabo.

The National Palace and the fountains of Montjuïc. ▷

Art National Museum (MNAC), which represents, through its collections, the history of Catalan art in different periods and, through its varied programme of activities, a view of the present situation of art in Catalonia. The MNAC contains collections of priceless manifestations of Romanesque, Gothic, Renaissance and baroque art.

Near to the National Palace as we make our way along Passeig de l'Exposició, between two museums of great interest, the **Ethnological and Archaeological Museums**, is the **Teatre Grec**, an amphitheatre built in the classical style after the Epidauran model, hidden amongst the vegetation of the site. Though it was little used after its construction in 1929, it has been revived in recent decades as the scene for a variety of cultural events.

Our visit to the mountain ends with the Montjuïc **"Magic Fountain"**, an illuminated fountain. Behind it are the buildings of the **Barcelona Trade Fair** («Fira de Barcelona») with, in the background, **Plaça d'Espanya** and **Les Arenes bullring**.

General view of the port of Barcelona.

A city overlooking the sea

One of the most important achievements of the city of Barcelona as part of the creation of new infrastructure for the 1992 Olympic Games was the recovery of the sea front. During the Industrial Revolution, many factories were constructed in the Port of Barcelona, but we can now admire a city open to the sea. The Port of Barcelona, now divided into the old and the new, the Port Vell and the Port Nou, has been regenerated as part of the latest initiatives. Few attractions in the Mediterranean have the charm of Port Vell, and it is in this modern spot that we find **Maremagnum**, a shopping, leisure and gastronomic centre situated in a privileged position over the Mediterranean Sea. The centre is reached by crossing the modern pedestrian «catwalk» known as the **Rambla del Mar**, which joins the statue of Columbus and the Rambla with Maremagnum. With area of 39,000 square metres, Maremagnum is the latest thing in shopping and leisure, with bars, terraces, boutiques, restaurants and even a minigolf. These leisure facilities are rounded off by the Maremagnum Cinemas. The Port Vell also contains the **Aquarium**, the largest in Europe and the most important in the world on the theme of the Mediterranean. In it, an 80-metre glass-walled tunnel runs through an immense circular oceanarium containing 4,000 specimens, including the star attraction - sharks. Next to the Aquarium, the **Imax** is found, a hall that combines three large-size projection systems: Imax, Omnimax and 3D. The cultural offering is completed by a visit to the **Catalan History Museum**, situated in the **Palau de Mar** (Sea Palace), in the emblematic neighborhood of Barceloneta.

On the other side of Maremagnum, we can see the new construction of the business center, **World Trade Center**, and a little further south, a large draw-

The Rambla de Mar and the Maremàgnum.

The Barcelona Aquarium.

bridge, called **Gate of Europe**, inaugurated in 2001.
Continuing towards Poble Nou is **Vila Olímpica**, a new neighborhood created for the '92 Olympics, which includes the **Olympic Port**, where two tall buildings stand out: the **Hotel Arts** and the **Mapfre Tower**. Their height, some 150 meters, is similar to the new **Agbar Tower** (2003), next to the square of Glories Catalanes, and only

Drawbridge known as "Door of Europe".

Olympic Port, and, in the background, the Mapfre Tower and Arts Hotel.

outdone in the city by the **Communications Tower of Collserola**, on the hillside of the Tibidabo.

Past the neighborhood of Poble Nou, the waterfront of Barcelona is completed by the enclosure of the **Forum**, the main setting for the international cultural date of the Forum Barcelona 2004. 30 totally renovated hectares have given place to one of the largest entertainment complexes in the world. Among the new constructions, the rectangular-

Virtual image of the Forum Building.
© Forum 2004 / Infrastructuras del Llevant S.A.

shaped **Forum Building**, the **Convention Center**, with capacity for 26,000 people, and a new marina stand out.

CONTENTS

Introduction...2

The Cathedral and the Gothic Quarter..4

Picasso Museum and carrer Montcada...15

The colourful Rambla 17

Sant Pau del Camp, the Monument to Columbus
and surrounding area 24

The Ciutadella, an oasis of green...28

Passeig de Gràcia: Modernist Barcelona......................................32

The Palau de la Música Catalana, home of culture 38

Pedralbes and Tibidabo, the heights of the city 41

The dreams of Gaudí: Park Güell and Sagrada Família..............44

Montjuïc and the Olympic Ring 50

A city overlooking the sea 58

Map of Barcelona 62

EDITORIAL ESCUDO DE ORO, S.A.
I.S.B.N. 84-378-1639-4
Printed by FISA - Escudo de Oro, S.A.
Legal Dep. B. 23708-2005

Protegemos el bosque; papel procedente de cultivos forestales controlados
Wir schützen den Wald. Papier aus kontrollierten Forsten.
We protect our forests. The paper used comes from controlled forestry plantations
Nous sauvegardons la forêt: papier provenant de cultures forestières controlées